# CONTENTS

Introduction
    Why Economics Matters
    Dispelling Myths
    The Goal of This Book
    How to Use This Book
    A Note on Humor
    Acknowledgments
Chapter 1: The Basics
    What is Economics?
    Microeconomics vs. Macroeconomics
    Supply and Demand
    Equilibrium
    Elasticity
    Opportunity Cost
    Marginal Analysis
    Incentives
    The Role of Assumptions
Chapter 2: Money Matters
    What is Money?
    The Evolution of Money
    Inflation and Deflation
    The Role of Central Banks
    Money Supply and Economic Health
    Cryptocurrencies and the Future of Money
Chapter 3: The Market

Types of Markets
　　　Market Structures
　　　Market Failures
　　　Government Intervention
　　　The Role of Prices
　　　Consumer and Producer Surplus
　Chapter 4: Government and the Economy
　　　Taxes and Spending
　　　Regulation and Deregulation
　　　Government Intervention in Markets
　　　Monetary Policy
　　　Economic Stabilization
　　　Income Redistribution
　Chapter 5: Personal Finance
　　　Budgeting 101
　　　Saving for Emergencies
　　　Managing Debt
　　　Investing for the Future
　　　Understanding Credit
　　　Insurance and Protection
　　　Retirement Planning
　　　Estate Planning
　Chapter 6: Global Economics
　　　Trade and Tariffs
　　　Globalization
　　　The Role of International Organizations
　　　Global Supply Chains
　　　Trade Agreements
　　　Foreign Direct Investment (FDI)
　　　Exchange Rates and Currency Markets
　　　Global Economic Challenges
　Chapter 7: Economic Indicators

- GDP, Unemployment, and Inflation
- Reading the News
- Leading, Lagging, and Coincident Indicators
- Other Key Economic Indicators
- Interpreting Economic Indicators

Chapter 8: Common Economic Fallacies
- Debunking Myths
- Fallacy 1: The Broken Window Fallacy
- Fallacy 2: Zero-Sum Thinking
- Fallacy 3: Post Hoc Ergo Propter Hoc
- Fallacy 4: The Lump of Labor Fallacy
- Fallacy 5: The Free Lunch Fallacy
- Fallacy 6: The Nirvana Fallacy
- Fallacy 7: The Sunk Cost Fallacy
- Fallacy 8: The Correlation-Causation Fallacy
- Fallacy 9: The Fallacy of the Single Cause
- Critical Thinking
- Questioning Assumptions
- Analyzing Trade-Offs
- Evaluating Evidence
- Understanding Incentives
- Thinking Systemically

Conclusion
- Why You're Not Stupid
- The Journey of Learning
- Applying What You've Learned
- Encouragement for Further Exploration
- Final Thoughts

Appendices
- Glossary of Terms
- Further Reading
- Useful Websites and Resources

# INTRODUCTION

## Why Economics Matters

Economics isn't just a subject for academics or policymakers; it's a vital part of everyday life. Whether you're deciding how to spend your paycheck, planning for retirement, or voting in an election, economic principles are at play. Understanding these principles can help you make better decisions, improve your financial well-being, and understand the world around you. Economics affects everything from the price of your morning coffee to the policies that shape our society.

## Dispelling Myths

Many people think economics is too complicated or irrelevant to their daily lives. This book aims to dispel those myths by breaking down complex concepts into simple, relatable terms. You don't need a degree to understand economics; you just need a willingness to learn. By the end of this book, you'll see that economics is not only accessible but also incredibly useful.

## The Goal of This Book

The goal of this book is to make economics approachable and engaging. We'll use everyday examples, humor, and straightforward explanations to help you grasp key concepts. Whether you're a student, a professional, or just someone curious about how the world works, this book is for you. We want to empower you with the knowledge to make informed decisions and understand the economic forces that shape your life.

## How to Use This Book

Each chapter is designed to build on the previous one, gradually increasing your understanding of economic principles. You can read the book from start to finish or jump to the chapters that interest you the most. We've included real-world examples, simple definitions, and practical tips to make the content as useful as possible.

## A Note on Humor

Economics can be a dry subject, but it doesn't have to be. We'll use humor and relatable scenarios to keep things light and engaging. After all, learning should be fun, and we believe that a good laugh can make even the most complex topics easier to understand.

## Acknowledgments

We'd like to thank all the teachers, economists, and everyday people who have contributed to our understanding of economics. Their insights and experiences have helped shape this book, and we hope to pass on their wisdom in a way that's both informative and enjoyable.

## Final Thoughts

Economics is a powerful tool that can help you navigate the complexities of the modern world. By understanding the basics, you'll be better equipped to make decisions that benefit you and those around you. So, let's dive in and discover the fascinating world of economics together. Remember, you're not stupid—you're just getting started on your journey to economic literacy.

# CHAPTER 1: THE BASICS

## What is Economics?

Economics is the study of how people use resources to satisfy their needs and wants. It involves making choices about what to produce, how to produce it, and who gets to consume it. At its core, economics is about decision-making and trade-offs. Every choice we make has an opportunity cost, which is the value of the next best alternative that we give up.

*Example:* If you decide to spend an hour watching TV, the opportunity cost might be the hour you could have spent studying or exercising.

## Microeconomics vs. Macroeconomics

Economics is divided into two main branches: microeconomics and macroeconomics. Microeconomics focuses on individual and business decisions, such as how much to produce or what price to charge. Macroeconomics looks at the economy as a whole, including issues like inflation, unemployment, and economic growth.

*Example:* Microeconomics might study how a single company sets its prices, while macroeconomics would examine how changes in interest rates affect the entire economy.

## Supply and Demand

Supply and demand are the fundamental forces that drive markets. The law of demand states that, all else being equal, as the price of a good or service decreases, the quantity demanded increases, and vice versa. The law of supply states that as the price of a good or service increases, the quantity supplied increases, and vice versa.

*Example:* Imagine a new smartphone is released. If everyone wants it but there are only a few available, the price will be high. If the company produces more phones and they become widely available, the price will drop.

## Equilibrium

The point where supply and demand meet is called equilibrium. At this point, the quantity of goods supplied equals the quantity demanded, and the market is in balance. Prices tend to stabilize at this point.

*Example:* If a bakery makes 100 loaves of bread and exactly 100 customers want to buy them at $2 each, the market is in equilibrium.

## Elasticity

Elasticity measures how much the quantity demanded or supplied responds to changes in price. If a small change in price leads to a large change in quantity demanded or supplied, the product is considered elastic. If a large change in price leads to a small change in quantity demanded or supplied, the product is inelastic.

*Example:* Luxury items like designer handbags are often elastic because a small price increase can lead to a significant drop in demand. Necessities like insulin are inelastic because people need them regardless of price changes.

## Opportunity Cost

Opportunity cost is the value of the next best alternative that you give up when you make a choice. It's a key concept in economics because it highlights the trade-offs involved in every decision.

*Example:* If you choose to spend $50 on a concert ticket, the opportunity cost might be the nice dinner you could have had instead.

## Marginal Analysis

Marginal analysis involves examining the additional benefits and costs of a decision. It's used to determine the optimal level of an activity.

*Example:* A company might use marginal analysis to decide how many units of a product to produce. If the marginal cost of producing one more unit is less than the marginal revenue from selling it, the company should produce more.

## Incentives

Incentives are factors that motivate people to act in certain ways. They can be positive (rewards) or negative (penalties).

*Example:* A tax credit for installing solar panels is a positive incentive to encourage renewable energy use. A fine for littering is a negative incentive to discourage pollution.

## The Role of Assumptions

Economists often use models to simplify complex real-world situations. These models rely on assumptions to make them manageable. While assumptions can sometimes oversimplify, they help economists focus on the most important factors.

*Example:* An economic model might assume that all other factors remain constant (ceteris paribus) to isolate the effect of a single variable.

# CHAPTER 2: MONEY MATTERS

## What is Money?

Money is a medium of exchange that facilitates trade by eliminating the inefficiencies of a barter system. It serves three primary functions: as a medium of exchange, a unit of account, and a store of value.

- **Medium of Exchange**: Money is widely accepted in exchange for goods and services.
- **Unit of Account**: Money provides a common measure for valuing goods and services.
- **Store of Value**: Money can be saved and retrieved in the future, retaining its value over time.

*Example:* In ancient times, people might have traded goods directly, like exchanging a cow for a sack of grain. Money simplifies this process by providing a common medium that everyone accepts.

## The Evolution of Money

Money has evolved significantly over time, from barter systems to coins, paper money, and now digital currencies.

- **Barter System**: Direct exchange of goods and services.
- **Commodity Money**: Items with intrinsic value, like gold or silver.
- **Fiat Money**: Currency without intrinsic value but

accepted by government decree.

- **Digital Money**: Electronic forms of money, including cryptocurrencies.

*Example:* Bitcoin is a type of digital currency that operates independently of a central bank, using blockchain technology to secure transactions.

## Inflation and Deflation

Inflation is the rate at which the general level of prices for goods and services rises, eroding purchasing power. Deflation is the opposite, where prices decrease over time, increasing purchasing power.

- **Causes of Inflation**: Demand-pull inflation (excess demand), cost-push inflation (rising production costs), and built-in inflation (wage-price spiral).
- **Effects of Inflation**: Reduced purchasing power, increased cost of living, and potential for hyperinflation.
- **Causes of Deflation**: Decreased demand, increased supply, and technological advancements.
- **Effects of Deflation**: Increased real value of debt, reduced consumer spending, and potential for economic stagnation.

*Example:* During hyperinflation in Zimbabwe in the late 2000s, prices doubled every day, making the local currency virtually worthless.

## The Role of Central Banks

Central banks, like the Federal Reserve in the United States, play a crucial role in managing a country's money supply and monetary policy. They aim to control inflation, stabilize the currency, and achieve full employment.

- **Monetary Policy Tools**: Interest rates, open market operations, and reserve requirements.

- **Interest Rates**: Central banks can raise or lower interest rates to influence borrowing and spending.
- **Open Market Operations**: Buying and selling government securities to control the money supply.
- **Reserve Requirements**: Setting the minimum reserves that banks must hold to ensure stability.

*Example:* During the 2008 financial crisis, the Federal Reserve lowered interest rates to near zero to encourage borrowing and stimulate the economy.

## Money Supply and Economic Health

The money supply, or the total amount of money in circulation, is a key indicator of economic health. It includes various measures, such as M1 (cash and checking deposits) and M2 (savings deposits, money market securities).

- **M1**: Highly liquid forms of money, including cash and checking deposits.
- **M2**: Includes M1 plus savings deposits, money market securities, and other near-money assets.

*Example:* An increase in the money supply can stimulate economic growth, but if it grows too quickly, it can lead to inflation.

## Cryptocurrencies and the Future of Money

Cryptocurrencies, like Bitcoin and Ethereum, represent a new frontier in the evolution of money. They offer decentralized, secure, and transparent transactions, but also come with challenges like volatility and regulatory concerns.

- **Blockchain Technology**: The underlying technology for most cryptocurrencies, providing a secure and transparent ledger.
- **Pros and Cons**: Cryptocurrencies offer benefits like lower transaction fees and increased privacy but face issues like price volatility and regulatory uncertainty.

*Example:* Bitcoin's value has seen significant fluctuations, rising from a few cents to over $60,000 per coin at its peak, highlighting both its potential and volatility.

# CHAPTER 3: THE MARKET

## Types of Markets

Markets are places where buyers and sellers come together to exchange goods and services. They can be physical locations, like a farmers' market, or virtual spaces, like online stores. Markets can also be categorized based on their scope and the nature of the goods and services traded.

- **Local Markets**: These are small-scale markets serving a specific community or region. Examples include farmers' markets and local craft fairs.

- **National Markets**: These markets operate within a single country and include national stock exchanges and large retail chains.

- **Global Markets**: These markets involve international trade and include global stock exchanges, multinational corporations, and online marketplaces like Amazon and Alibaba.

*Example:* The New York Stock Exchange (NYSE) is a national market, while eBay operates as a global market where people from different countries can buy and sell goods.

## Market Structures

Markets can also be classified based on their structure, which affects how prices are determined and how competition operates.

- **Perfect Competition**: A market structure where many

small firms sell identical products, and no single firm can influence the market price. There are no barriers to entry or exit.

- **Monopolistic Competition**: A market structure where many firms sell similar but not identical products. Each firm has some control over its prices due to product differentiation.

- **Oligopoly**: A market structure where a few large firms dominate the market. These firms may collude to set prices or output levels.

- **Monopoly**: A market structure where a single firm controls the entire market. This firm has significant control over prices and can set them to maximize profits.

*Example:* The fast-food industry is an example of monopolistic competition, with many firms offering similar but differentiated products. The utility industry, like electricity providers, often operates as a monopoly in a given region.

## Market Failures

Sometimes markets don't work perfectly, leading to inefficiencies known as market failures. These failures occur when the allocation of goods and services is not optimal, resulting in wasted resources or unmet needs.

- **Externalities**: Costs or benefits of a transaction that affect third parties who are not involved in the transaction. Externalities can be positive (benefits) or negative (costs).

- **Public Goods**: Goods that are non-excludable and non-rivalrous, meaning they can be used by everyone without reducing their availability to others. Examples include clean air and national defense.

- **Information Asymmetry**: A situation where one

party in a transaction has more or better information than the other, leading to an imbalance in decision-making.

- **Monopolies and Oligopolies**: When a single firm or a few firms dominate a market, they can restrict output and raise prices, leading to inefficiencies.

*Example:* Pollution is a negative externality where the market fails to account for the environmental costs of production. Vaccinations are a positive externality because they provide herd immunity, benefiting even those who are not vaccinated.

## Government Intervention

Governments often intervene in markets to correct failures and promote efficiency and equity. This intervention can take various forms, including regulations, subsidies, taxes, and public provision of goods and services.

- **Regulations**: Rules set by the government to control how businesses operate. These can include safety standards, environmental protections, and labor laws.
- **Subsidies**: Financial assistance provided by the government to encourage the production or consumption of certain goods and services.
- **Taxes**: Levies imposed by the government on goods, services, and income to raise revenue and discourage certain behaviors.
- **Public Goods Provision**: The government may provide goods and services that the market fails to supply efficiently, such as public education and infrastructure.

*Example:* The government may impose a carbon tax to reduce greenhouse gas emissions or provide subsidies for renewable energy projects to encourage their development.

## The Role of Prices

Prices play a crucial role in markets by signaling information to buyers and sellers. They help allocate resources efficiently by reflecting the relative scarcity and value of goods and services.

- **Price Signals**: Prices convey information about the supply and demand for goods and services. High prices indicate scarcity and encourage producers to supply more, while low prices indicate abundance and encourage consumers to buy more.
- **Price Mechanism**: The process by which prices adjust to balance supply and demand. When demand exceeds supply, prices rise, and when supply exceeds demand, prices fall.

*Example:* During a natural disaster, the price of bottled water may rise due to increased demand and limited supply, signaling the need for more production and distribution.

## Consumer and Producer Surplus

Consumer and producer surplus are measures of the economic benefits that buyers and sellers receive from participating in a market.

- **Consumer Surplus**: The difference between what consumers are willing to pay for a good or service and what they actually pay. It represents the extra satisfaction or utility gained by consumers.
- **Producer Surplus**: The difference between what producers are willing to accept for a good or service and what they actually receive. It represents the extra profit or benefit gained by producers.

*Example:* If a consumer is willing to pay $10 for a product but buys it for $7, the consumer surplus is $3. If a producer is willing to sell a product for $5 but sells it for $7, the producer surplus is $2.

# CHAPTER 4: GOVERNMENT AND THE ECONOMY

## Taxes and Spending

Governments collect taxes to fund public services and infrastructure, such as education, healthcare, roads, and national defense. The way a government collects and spends money can significantly impact the economy.

- **Types of Taxes**: Taxes can be direct (income tax, property tax) or indirect (sales tax, value-added tax). Progressive taxes increase with income, while regressive taxes take a larger percentage from lower-income individuals.

- **Government Spending**: Public spending can be categorized into mandatory spending (entitlements like Social Security and Medicare) and discretionary spending (defense, education, infrastructure).

- **Fiscal Policy**: The use of government spending and taxation to influence the economy. Expansionary fiscal policy involves increasing spending or cutting taxes to stimulate the economy, while contractionary fiscal policy involves reducing spending or increasing taxes to cool down an overheated economy.

*Example:* During a recession, the government might implement an expansionary fiscal policy by increasing infrastructure spending to create jobs and stimulate economic activity.

## Regulation and Deregulation

Regulations are rules set by the government to control how businesses operate. They aim to protect consumers, workers, and the environment, but they can also impact business efficiency and innovation.

- **Types of Regulations**: Regulations can cover a wide range of areas, including environmental protection, labor standards, consumer safety, and financial practices.

- **Benefits of Regulation**: Regulations can prevent harmful practices, ensure fair competition, and protect public health and safety.

- **Costs of Regulation**: Excessive regulation can stifle innovation, increase costs for businesses, and reduce economic efficiency.

- **Deregulation**: The process of removing or reducing government regulations to allow for more competition and innovation. While deregulation can boost economic growth, it can also lead to negative consequences if not managed properly.

*Example:* The deregulation of the airline industry in the United States in the late 1970s led to increased competition, lower fares, and more choices for consumers, but also resulted in some negative outcomes like reduced service quality and financial instability for some airlines.

## Government Intervention in Markets

Governments intervene in markets to correct market failures, promote economic stability, and achieve social goals. This intervention can take various forms, including subsidies, price controls, and public provision of goods and services.

- **Subsidies**: Financial assistance provided by the

government to support specific industries or activities. Subsidies can help promote economic development, support struggling industries, and encourage positive externalities.

- **Price Controls**: Government-imposed limits on the prices that can be charged for goods and services. Price ceilings prevent prices from rising too high, while price floors prevent prices from falling too low.

- **Public Goods Provision**: The government may provide goods and services that the market fails to supply efficiently, such as public education, healthcare, and infrastructure.

*Example:* Rent control is a type of price ceiling that aims to make housing more affordable, but it can also lead to reduced supply and quality of rental properties.

## Monetary Policy

Monetary policy involves managing the money supply and interest rates to influence economic activity. Central banks, like the Federal Reserve in the United States, are responsible for implementing monetary policy.

- **Interest Rates**: Central banks can raise or lower interest rates to influence borrowing and spending. Lowering interest rates makes borrowing cheaper and encourages spending, while raising interest rates makes borrowing more expensive and encourages saving.

- **Open Market Operations**: The buying and selling of government securities to control the money supply. When the central bank buys securities, it increases the money supply; when it sells securities, it decreases the money supply.

- **Quantitative Easing**: A form of monetary policy where the central bank buys long-term securities to increase the money supply and lower interest rates, stimulating economic activity.

*Example:* During the 2008 financial crisis, the Federal Reserve implemented quantitative easing to inject liquidity into the financial system and support economic recovery.

## Economic Stabilization

Governments use fiscal and monetary policies to stabilize the economy and mitigate the effects of economic cycles. These policies aim to smooth out fluctuations in economic activity and maintain stable growth.

- **Countercyclical Policies**: Policies that counteract economic fluctuations. During a recession, expansionary policies are used to stimulate growth, while during a boom, contractionary policies are used to prevent overheating.
- **Automatic Stabilizers**: Economic policies and programs that automatically adjust to changes in economic conditions without the need for explicit government action. Examples include unemployment insurance and progressive tax systems.

*Example:* Unemployment benefits act as an automatic stabilizer by providing income support to unemployed workers, helping to maintain consumer spending during economic downturns.

## Income Redistribution

Governments often implement policies to redistribute income and reduce economic inequality. These policies aim to ensure a more equitable distribution of wealth and resources.

- **Progressive Taxation**: A tax system where higher-income individuals pay a larger percentage of their income in taxes. This helps to reduce income inequality and fund public services.

- **Social Welfare Programs**: Government programs that provide financial assistance and support to individuals and families in need. Examples include Social Security, Medicaid, and food assistance programs.
- **Minimum Wage Laws**: Regulations that set the lowest wage that employers can legally pay their workers. Minimum wage laws aim to ensure a basic standard of living for low-income workers.

*Example:* The Earned Income Tax Credit (EITC) in the United States is a refundable tax credit that provides financial support to low- and moderate-income working families, helping to reduce poverty and encourage work.

# CHAPTER 5: PERSONAL FINANCE

## Budgeting 101

Budgeting is the cornerstone of personal finance. It involves planning your income and expenses to ensure you live within your means and achieve your financial goals.

- **Track Your Income and Expenses**: Start by recording all sources of income and tracking your spending. This helps you understand where your money is going and identify areas where you can cut back.

- **Set Financial Goals**: Define short-term and long-term financial goals, such as saving for a vacation, paying off debt, or building an emergency fund.

- **Create a Budget Plan**: Allocate your income to different categories, such as housing, food, transportation, savings, and entertainment. Use budgeting tools or apps to help you stay on track.

- **Adjust as Needed**: Review your budget regularly and make adjustments based on changes in your income or expenses.

*Example:* If you find that you're spending too much on dining out, you can set a limit for restaurant expenses and allocate more money towards savings.

## Saving for Emergencies

An emergency fund is essential for financial security. It provides a safety net for unexpected expenses, such as medical bills, car repairs, or job loss.

- **Determine Your Savings Goal**: Aim to save at least three to six months' worth of living expenses. This amount can vary based on your personal circumstances and job stability.
- **Automate Your Savings**: Set up automatic transfers to a separate savings account to ensure you consistently save a portion of your income.
- **Keep It Accessible**: Store your emergency fund in a high-yield savings account that is easily accessible but separate from your regular checking account.

*Example:* If your monthly expenses are $2,000, aim to save between $6,000 and $12,000 in your emergency fund.

## Managing Debt

Managing debt effectively is crucial for financial health. High levels of debt can lead to financial stress and limit your ability to save and invest.

- **Understand Your Debt**: List all your debts, including credit cards, student loans, and mortgages. Note the interest rates, minimum payments, and due dates.
- **Prioritize High-Interest Debt**: Focus on paying off high-interest debt first, as it can accumulate quickly and become more expensive over time.
- **Consider Debt Repayment Strategies**: Use methods like the debt snowball (paying off the smallest debts first) or the debt avalanche (paying off the highest interest debts first) to tackle your debt systematically.
- **Avoid New Debt**: Limit the use of credit cards and avoid taking on new debt unless absolutely necessary.

*Example:* If you have a credit card with a 20% interest rate and a student loan with a 5% interest rate, prioritize paying off the credit card debt first.

## Investing for the Future

Investing is a key component of building wealth and achieving long-term financial goals. It involves putting your money to work to generate returns over time.

- **Understand Different Investment Options**: Common investment options include stocks, bonds, mutual funds, real estate, and retirement accounts like 401(k)s and IRAs.
- **Diversify Your Portfolio**: Spread your investments across different asset classes to reduce risk and increase potential returns.
- **Start Early**: The earlier you start investing, the more time your money has to grow through the power of compound interest.
- **Seek Professional Advice**: Consider consulting a financial advisor to help you create an investment strategy that aligns with your goals and risk tolerance.

*Example:* If you invest $5,000 annually in a retirement account with an average annual return of 7%, you could have over $500,000 after 30 years.

## Understanding Credit

Your credit score is a crucial factor in your financial health. It affects your ability to borrow money, rent an apartment, and even get a job.

- **Check Your Credit Report**: Regularly review your credit report to ensure accuracy and identify any errors or fraudulent activity.
- **Pay Bills on Time**: Timely payments are one of the most significant factors affecting your credit score.

- **Keep Credit Utilization Low**: Aim to use less than 30% of your available credit to maintain a healthy credit score.
- **Avoid Opening Too Many Accounts**: Each new credit application can temporarily lower your credit score, so be selective about applying for new credit.

*Example:* If you have a credit card with a $10,000 limit, try to keep your balance below $3,000 to maintain a good credit utilization ratio.

## Insurance and Protection

Insurance is essential for protecting yourself and your assets from unexpected events. It provides financial security and peace of mind.

- **Types of Insurance**: Common types of insurance include health, auto, home, life, and disability insurance.
- **Assess Your Needs**: Determine the types and amounts of insurance coverage you need based on your personal circumstances and financial goals.
- **Shop Around**: Compare insurance policies and providers to find the best coverage at the most affordable price.
- **Review Regularly**: Periodically review your insurance coverage to ensure it still meets your needs and make adjustments as necessary.

*Example:* If you own a home, homeowners insurance can protect you from financial loss due to damage or theft.

## Retirement Planning

Planning for retirement is essential to ensure you have enough money to support yourself in your later years.

- **Estimate Your Retirement Needs**: Calculate how

much money you'll need to maintain your desired lifestyle in retirement. Consider factors like living expenses, healthcare costs, and inflation.

- **Contribute to Retirement Accounts**: Take advantage of employer-sponsored retirement plans like 401(k)s and individual retirement accounts (IRAs). Contribute regularly and take advantage of any employer matching contributions.

- **Diversify Your Investments**: Spread your retirement savings across different asset classes to reduce risk and increase potential returns.

- **Monitor and Adjust**: Regularly review your retirement plan and make adjustments based on changes in your financial situation and goals.

*Example:* If you plan to retire at age 65 and expect to live until age 85, you'll need to save enough to cover 20 years of living expenses.

## Estate Planning

Estate planning involves preparing for the transfer of your assets after your death. It ensures your wishes are carried out and can help minimize taxes and legal complications for your heirs.

- **Create a Will**: A will outlines how you want your assets distributed and who will care for any minor children.

- **Establish a Trust**: Trusts can provide more control over how your assets are distributed and can help avoid probate.

- **Designate Beneficiaries**: Ensure your retirement accounts, life insurance policies, and other financial accounts have designated beneficiaries.

- **Plan for Incapacity**: Consider creating a power of attorney and a healthcare directive to outline your wishes if you become unable to make decisions for yourself.

*Example:* A living trust can help ensure your assets are distributed according to your wishes without the need for probate, which can be time-consuming and costly.

# CHAPTER 6: GLOBAL ECONOMICS

## Trade and Tariffs

International trade involves the exchange of goods and services between countries. It allows countries to specialize in the production of goods and services they can produce most efficiently, leading to increased economic welfare.

- **Comparative Advantage**: The principle that countries should specialize in producing goods where they have a lower opportunity cost compared to other countries. This leads to more efficient global production and trade.
- **Benefits of Trade**: Trade can lead to lower prices for consumers, access to a wider variety of goods and services, and increased economic growth.
- **Tariffs and Trade Barriers**: Tariffs are taxes imposed on imported goods, making them more expensive and less competitive compared to domestic products. Other trade barriers include quotas, subsidies, and import restrictions.

*Example:* If Country A can produce wine more efficiently than cheese, and Country B can produce cheese more efficiently than wine, both countries benefit by trading wine for cheese.

## Globalization

Globalization refers to the increasing interconnectedness of economies, cultures, and populations across the world. It has significant economic, social, and political implications.

- **Economic Globalization**: The integration of national economies through trade, investment, and capital flows. It includes the rise of multinational corporations and global supply chains.
- **Cultural Globalization**: The spread of ideas, values, and cultural products across borders. This can lead to greater cultural exchange but also concerns about cultural homogenization.
- **Political Globalization**: The increasing influence of international organizations and agreements on national policies. Examples include the United Nations, World Trade Organization, and regional trade agreements.

*Example:* The rise of the internet and digital communication has accelerated globalization by making it easier for people and businesses to connect and collaborate across borders.

## The Role of International Organizations

International organizations play a crucial role in facilitating global trade, promoting economic stability, and addressing global challenges.

- **World Trade Organization (WTO)**: The WTO oversees global trade rules and helps resolve trade disputes between countries. It aims to promote free and fair trade by reducing trade barriers.
- **International Monetary Fund (IMF)**: The IMF provides financial assistance and advice to countries facing economic instability. It aims to promote global monetary cooperation and financial stability.
- **World Bank**: The World Bank provides financial and technical assistance to developing countries for

development projects that aim to reduce poverty and promote sustainable development.

*Example:* The WTO helped mediate a trade dispute between the United States and China, leading to an agreement that reduced tariffs and improved trade relations.

## Global Supply Chains

Global supply chains involve the production and distribution of goods across multiple countries. They allow businesses to take advantage of lower production costs and access new markets.

- **Benefits of Global Supply Chains**: Cost savings, increased efficiency, and access to a broader range of resources and markets.
- **Challenges of Global Supply Chains**: Supply chain disruptions, geopolitical risks, and ethical concerns related to labor practices and environmental impact.

*Example:* A smartphone might be designed in the United States, manufactured in China, and assembled with components from various countries, illustrating the complexity of global supply chains.

## Trade Agreements

Trade agreements are treaties between countries that facilitate trade by reducing or eliminating trade barriers. They can be bilateral (between two countries) or multilateral (involving multiple countries).

- **Free Trade Agreements (FTAs)**: Agreements that aim to eliminate tariffs and other trade barriers between member countries. Examples include the North American Free Trade Agreement (NAFTA) and the European Union (EU).
- **Regional Trade Agreements**: Agreements between countries in a specific region to promote economic integration and cooperation. Examples include the

Association of Southeast Asian Nations (ASEAN) and the African Continental Free Trade Area (AfCFTA).

*Example:* The Comprehensive and Progressive Agreement for Trans-Pacific Partnership (CPTPP) is a multilateral trade agreement that aims to promote trade and investment among its member countries in the Asia-Pacific region.

## Foreign Direct Investment (FDI)

Foreign direct investment involves investing in a foreign country by establishing business operations or acquiring business assets. FDI can drive economic growth, create jobs, and transfer technology and skills.

- **Types of FDI**: Greenfield investment (establishing new operations) and brownfield investment (acquiring existing operations).
- **Benefits of FDI**: Economic growth, job creation, and technology transfer.
- **Challenges of FDI**: Political and economic risks, cultural differences, and potential negative impacts on local businesses and communities.

*Example:* A multinational corporation like Toyota might build a new manufacturing plant in the United States, creating jobs and contributing to the local economy.

## Exchange Rates and Currency Markets

Exchange rates determine the value of one currency relative to another. They play a crucial role in international trade and investment.

- **Factors Influencing Exchange Rates**: Interest rates, inflation, political stability, and economic performance.
- **Types of Exchange Rate Systems**: Fixed exchange rate (pegged to another currency) and floating exchange rate (determined by market forces).

- **Impact of Exchange Rates**: Exchange rate fluctuations can affect the competitiveness of exports and imports, as well as the value of foreign investments.

*Example:* If the US dollar strengthens against the euro, American goods become more expensive for European consumers, potentially reducing US exports to Europe.

## Global Economic Challenges

Globalization and international trade bring numerous benefits, but they also pose significant challenges that require coordinated efforts to address.

- **Income Inequality**: Globalization can lead to increased income inequality within and between countries. Addressing this issue requires policies that promote inclusive growth and equitable distribution of benefits.

- **Environmental Sustainability**: Economic growth and industrialization can lead to environmental degradation. Sustainable development practices and international cooperation are essential to address climate change and protect natural resources.

- **Global Health**: Pandemics and health crises can have severe economic and social impacts. Strengthening global health systems and cooperation is crucial to prevent and respond to health emergencies.

*Example:* The COVID-19 pandemic highlighted the interconnectedness of global economies and the need for coordinated responses to health crises and economic recovery.

# CHAPTER 7: ECONOMIC INDICATORS

## GDP, Unemployment, and Inflation

Economic indicators are statistics that provide insights into the health and performance of an economy. Three of the most important indicators are Gross Domestic Product (GDP), unemployment rates, and inflation.

- **Gross Domestic Product (GDP)**: GDP measures the total value of all goods and services produced within a country over a specific period, usually a year or a quarter. It is a key indicator of economic activity and growth.
    - **Real vs. Nominal GDP**: Nominal GDP is measured at current market prices, while real GDP is adjusted for inflation, providing a more accurate reflection of economic growth.
    - **GDP Per Capita**: This measures the average economic output per person, providing insights into the standard of living and economic well-being of a population.

*Example:* If a country's GDP grows by 3% in a year, it indicates that the economy is expanding and producing more goods and services.

- **Unemployment Rate**: The unemployment rate

measures the percentage of the labor force that is actively seeking work but is unable to find employment. It is a key indicator of labor market health.

- **Types of Unemployment:**
  - **Frictional Unemployment:** Short-term unemployment that occurs when people are between jobs or entering the labor force for the first time.
  - **Structural Unemployment:** Long-term unemployment resulting from changes in the economy, such as technological advancements or shifts in consumer demand.
  - **Cyclical Unemployment:** Unemployment caused by economic downturns or recessions.
- **Natural Rate of Unemployment:** The level of unemployment that exists when the economy is at full employment, accounting for frictional and structural unemployment.

*Example:* During a recession, the unemployment rate typically rises as businesses reduce their workforce in response to decreased demand.

- **Inflation:** Inflation measures the rate at which the general level of prices for goods and services rises, eroding purchasing power. It is typically measured by the Consumer Price Index (CPI) or the Producer Price Index (PPI).
  - **Causes of Inflation:**
    - **Demand-Pull Inflation:** Occurs when demand for goods and services exceeds supply, driving

up prices.
- **Cost-Push Inflation**: Occurs when production costs increase, leading to higher prices for goods and services.
- **Built-In Inflation**: Results from a wage-price spiral, where higher wages lead to higher production costs and, consequently, higher prices.
  - **Hyperinflation**: An extremely high and typically accelerating rate of inflation, often exceeding 50% per month.

*Example:* If the inflation rate is 2%, it means that, on average, prices for goods and services are 2% higher than they were a year ago.

## Reading the News

Understanding economic news can help you make informed decisions about your finances, investments, and career. Here are some tips for interpreting economic news:

- **Look for Trends**: Pay attention to trends over time rather than focusing on single data points. Trends can provide a clearer picture of the overall economic direction.
- **Consider the Source**: Evaluate the credibility and reliability of the news source. Reputable sources are more likely to provide accurate and unbiased information.
- **Understand the Context**: Economic indicators are influenced by various factors, including government policies, global events, and market conditions. Consider the broader context when interpreting economic news.
- **Be Skeptical of Predictions**: Economic forecasts are

often based on assumptions and models that may not always be accurate. Use predictions as one piece of information rather than relying on them entirely.

*Example:* If you read that the unemployment rate has decreased, consider whether this is part of a longer-term trend or a short-term fluctuation.

## Leading, Lagging, and Coincident Indicators

Economic indicators can be classified into three categories based on their timing relative to economic cycles: leading, lagging, and coincident indicators.

- **Leading Indicators**: These indicators predict future economic activity and are used to forecast economic trends. Examples include stock market performance, new business orders, and consumer confidence.

- **Lagging Indicators**: These indicators reflect past economic activity and are used to confirm trends. Examples include unemployment rates, corporate profits, and interest rates.

- **Coincident Indicators**: These indicators move in line with the overall economy and provide a snapshot of current economic conditions. Examples include GDP, industrial production, and retail sales.

*Example:* The stock market is a leading indicator because it often reacts to expectations about future economic conditions, while the unemployment rate is a lagging indicator because it reflects changes that have already occurred in the economy.

## Other Key Economic Indicators

In addition to GDP, unemployment, and inflation, several other indicators provide valuable insights into economic performance:

- **Consumer Confidence Index (CCI)**: Measures the level of optimism or pessimism that consumers feel about the overall state of the economy and their personal financial situation. High consumer confidence typically indicates increased consumer spending.

- **Producer Price Index (PPI)**: Measures the average change in selling prices received by domestic producers for their output. It is an indicator of inflation at the wholesale level.
- **Retail Sales**: Measures the total receipts of retail stores and provides insights into consumer spending patterns. It is a key indicator of consumer demand and economic health.
- **Industrial Production**: Measures the output of the industrial sector, including manufacturing, mining, and utilities. It provides insights into the strength of the industrial economy.
- **Housing Starts**: Measures the number of new residential construction projects that have begun. It is an indicator of the health of the housing market and overall economic activity.

*Example:* A rise in housing starts indicates increased construction activity, which can boost economic growth through job creation and increased demand for building materials.

## Interpreting Economic Indicators

Interpreting economic indicators requires understanding their significance and how they interact with each other. Here are some tips for making sense of economic data:

- **Compare with Historical Data**: Look at historical trends to understand how current data compares to past performance. This can help identify patterns and potential turning points.
- **Consider Seasonal Adjustments**: Many economic indicators are seasonally adjusted to account for

regular fluctuations, such as holiday shopping or agricultural cycles. Be aware of these adjustments when interpreting data.

- **Analyze Multiple Indicators**: Relying on a single indicator can be misleading. Consider a range of indicators to get a comprehensive view of economic conditions.

- **Stay Informed**: Keep up with economic news and reports from reputable sources. Understanding the latest data and trends can help you make informed decisions.

*Example:* If GDP growth is strong but consumer confidence is declining, it may indicate underlying concerns about future economic conditions.

# CHAPTER 8: COMMON ECONOMIC FALLACIES

## Debunking Myths

Many economic fallacies persist because they seem intuitive but are actually misleading. This chapter will debunk common myths and explain why they're wrong.

## Fallacy 1: The Broken Window Fallacy

The broken window fallacy suggests that economic activity resulting from repairing damage (like a broken window) is beneficial because it creates jobs and stimulates spending. However, this fallacy ignores the opportunity cost of the resources used for repairs.

- **Explanation**: When a window is broken, the money spent on repairs could have been used for other productive purposes, such as investing in new equipment or starting a new project. The fallacy overlooks the lost opportunities and the fact that no new wealth is created.
- **Example**: If a shopkeeper spends $100 to fix a broken window, that $100 could have been spent on new inventory or marketing, which might have generated more revenue.

## Fallacy 2: Zero-Sum Thinking

Zero-sum thinking assumes that one person's gain is another person's loss, implying that wealth and resources are fixed. In reality, economic growth and trade can create new wealth and opportunities, benefiting multiple parties.

- **Explanation**: Trade and economic activity can lead to mutual benefits, where both parties gain from the exchange. Economic growth can expand the overall pie, allowing for increased prosperity.
- **Example**: When two countries trade, both can benefit from access to goods and services that they cannot produce as efficiently on their own.

## Fallacy 3: Post Hoc Ergo Propter Hoc

This fallacy assumes that if one event follows another, the first event must have caused the second. In economics, this can lead to incorrect conclusions about causality.

- **Explanation**: Just because two events occur in sequence does not mean one caused the other. Correlation does not imply causation, and other factors may be at play.
- **Example**: If a government implements a new policy and the economy improves, it does not necessarily mean the policy caused the improvement. Other factors, such as global economic conditions, may have contributed.

## Fallacy 4: The Lump of Labor Fallacy

The lump of labor fallacy assumes that there is a fixed amount of work to be done in the economy, and that new workers (such as immigrants) will take jobs away from existing workers.

- **Explanation**: The economy is dynamic, and the amount of work is not fixed. New workers can create new demand for goods and services, leading to job creation and economic growth.
- **Example**: Immigrants may start new businesses, create jobs, and increase demand for housing, education, and other services, contributing to overall

economic growth.

## Fallacy 5: The Free Lunch Fallacy

The free lunch fallacy assumes that it is possible to get something for nothing, ignoring the costs and trade-offs involved.

- **Explanation**: Every economic decision involves trade-offs and opportunity costs. Resources are limited, and using them for one purpose means they cannot be used for another.
- **Example**: Government programs that provide "free" services, such as healthcare or education, are funded by taxes. The cost is borne by taxpayers, and there are trade-offs in how those resources are allocated.

## Fallacy 6: The Nirvana Fallacy

The Nirvana Fallacy occurs when people reject a realistic solution because it is not perfect, comparing it to an idealized, unattainable alternative.

- **Explanation**: This fallacy dismisses practical solutions by comparing them to perfect but unrealistic alternatives. It ignores that improvements, even if not perfect, are often valuable.
- **Example**: Rejecting a new law aimed at reducing pollution because it doesn't eliminate all pollution is an example of the Nirvana Fallacy. The law can still significantly improve air quality even if it isn't perfect[12].

## Fallacy 7: The Sunk Cost Fallacy

The Sunk Cost Fallacy is the tendency to continue an endeavor once an investment in money, effort, or time has been made, even when it would be more rational to abandon it.

- **Explanation**: This fallacy occurs because people feel that they have invested too much to quit, even if continuing is not in their best interest. Rational decision-making should ignore sunk costs and focus on future benefits and costs.

- **Example**: Continuing to invest in a failing project because significant resources have already been spent, rather than cutting losses and reallocating resources to more promising opportunities[34].

## Fallacy 8: The Correlation-Causation Fallacy

The Correlation-Causation Fallacy assumes that because two events occur together, one must cause the other.

- **Explanation**: Correlation does not imply causation. Two events may be correlated due to coincidence, a third factor causing both, or other reasons. Establishing causation requires more rigorous analysis.

- **Example**: Observing that ice cream sales and drowning incidents both increase in the summer does not mean ice cream consumption causes drowning. Both are influenced by the warmer weather[56].

## Fallacy 9: The Fallacy of the Single Cause

The Fallacy of the Single Cause assumes that a single factor is the sole cause of an outcome, ignoring the complexity of multiple contributing factors.

- **Explanation**: Most events are the result of multiple interacting causes. Oversimplifying to a single cause can lead to misunderstandings and ineffective solutions.

- **Example**: Attributing economic growth solely to a tax cut ignores other factors like technological advancements, consumer confidence, and global market conditions[78].

# Critical Thinking

Learning to think like an economist involves questioning assumptions and looking at the bigger picture. It's about being skeptical of easy answers and understanding the complexities of economic issues.

## Questioning Assumptions

- **Identify Assumptions**: Recognize the assumptions underlying economic arguments and policies. Question whether these assumptions are valid and consider alternative perspectives.

- **Challenge Simplistic Explanations**: Be wary of explanations that seem too simple or one-sided. Economic issues are often complex and multifaceted.

*Example*: When evaluating a policy proposal, consider the assumptions about human behavior, market conditions, and potential unintended consequences.

## Analyzing Trade-Offs

- **Opportunity Cost**: Always consider the opportunity cost of economic decisions. What are the alternatives, and what are the potential benefits and costs of each option?

- **Cost-Benefit Analysis**: Weigh the costs and benefits of different choices. Consider both short-term and long-term impacts, as well as direct and indirect effects.

*Example*: When deciding whether to invest in a new project, analyze the potential returns and risks, as well as the opportunity cost of not investing in other opportunities.

## Evaluating Evidence

- **Data and Statistics**: Use data and statistics to support or refute economic arguments. Be critical of the sources and methods used to collect and interpret data.
- **Case Studies and Examples**: Look at real-world examples and case studies to understand how economic principles apply in practice. Learn from both successes and failures.

*Example*: When assessing the impact of a minimum wage increase, examine empirical studies and data from different regions and time periods to understand the potential effects on employment and income.

## Understanding Incentives

- **Behavioral Responses**: Recognize that people respond to incentives. Consider how changes in policies or market conditions might influence behavior.
- **Unintended Consequences**: Be aware of potential unintended consequences of economic decisions. Policies designed to achieve one goal may have unexpected effects in other areas.

*Example*: A tax on sugary drinks may reduce consumption but could also lead to increased consumption of other unhealthy products or impact low-income households disproportionately.

## Thinking Systemically

- **Interconnectedness**: Understand that economic systems are interconnected. Changes in one part of the economy can have ripple effects throughout the system.
- **Feedback Loops**: Consider feedback loops, where changes in economic conditions can reinforce or counteract each other.

*Example*: A rise in interest rates can reduce borrowing and spending, leading to slower economic growth, which in turn can influence future interest rate decisions.

# CONCLUSION

## Why You're Not Stupid

Economics can seem daunting, but with the right approach, anyone can understand it. This book aims to empower you with the knowledge to make better decisions and understand the world around you. Remember, economics is not just about numbers and graphs; it's about people, choices, and the impact of those choices on our daily lives.

## The Journey of Learning

Understanding economics is a journey, not a destination. As you continue to learn and explore, you'll find that economics touches every aspect of life, from the prices you pay at the grocery store to the policies that shape our society. Keep questioning, keep learning, and keep applying economic principles to make informed decisions.

## Applying What You've Learned

Now that you've gained a foundational understanding of economics, you can apply these principles to various aspects of your life. Whether it's managing your personal finances, making informed voting decisions, or understanding global economic trends, the knowledge you've acquired will serve you well.

## Encouragement for Further Exploration

Don't stop here. Economics is a vast and ever-evolving field with much more to explore. Continue reading, discussing, and thinking critically about economic issues. Engage with different perspectives and stay curious. The more you learn, the more empowered you'll be to navigate the complexities of the modern world.

# FINAL THOUGHTS

Economics is a powerful tool that can help you navigate the complexities of the modern world. By understanding the basics, you'll be better equipped to make decisions that benefit you and those around you. So, let's dive in and discover the fascinating world of economics together. Remember, you're not stupid—you're just getting started on your journey to economic literacy.

# APPENDICES

## Glossary of Terms

Here are some key economic terms and their definitions to help you navigate the concepts discussed in the book:

- **Aggregate Demand**: The total demand for goods and services within an economy.
- **Balance of Trade**: The difference between the value of a country's exports and imports.
- **Capital**: Assets used for the production of goods and services, such as machinery, buildings, and equipment.
- **Deflation**: A decrease in the general price level of goods and services.
- **Elasticity**: A measure of how much the quantity demanded or supplied of a good responds to changes in price.
- **Fiscal Policy**: Government policies related to taxation and spending to influence the economy.
- **Gross Domestic Product (GDP)**: The total value of all goods and services produced within a country over a specific period.
- **Inflation**: An increase in the general price level of goods and services.
- **Monetary Policy**: Central bank policies related to the money supply and interest rates to influence the

economy.

- **Opportunity Cost**: The value of the next best alternative that is forgone when making a decision.
- **Supply and Demand**: The relationship between the quantity of a good or service that producers are willing to sell and the quantity that consumers are willing to buy.

## Further Reading

For those who want to dive deeper into economics, here are some recommended books and resources:

- **"Economics in One Lesson" by Henry Hazlitt**: A classic introduction to economic principles, focusing on the long-term consequences of economic decisions.
- **"Freakonomics" by Steven D. Levitt and Stephen J. Dubner**: An engaging exploration of economic concepts through unconventional questions and real-world examples.
- **"The Wealth of Nations" by Adam Smith**: A foundational text in economics that explores the nature and causes of economic prosperity.
- **"Capital in the Twenty-First Century" by Thomas Piketty**: An in-depth analysis of wealth inequality and its implications for the modern economy.
- **"Nudge" by Richard H. Thaler and Cass R. Sunstein**: A look at how behavioral economics can influence decision-making and public policy.
- **Online Courses**: Websites like Coursera, edX, and Khan Academy offer free and paid courses on various economic topics, taught by experts from top universities.

## Useful Websites and Resources

- **Federal Reserve (www.federalreserve.gov)**: Information on U.S. monetary policy, economic research, and data.

- **Bureau of Economic Analysis (www.bea.gov)**: Economic statistics and analysis, including GDP and personal income data.

- **World Bank (www.worldbank.org)**: Global economic data, research, and development projects.

- **International Monetary Fund (www.imf.org)**: Global economic analysis, financial assistance, and policy advice.

- **Investopedia (www.investopedia.com)**: Articles, tutorials, and resources on a wide range of economic and financial topics.

www.ingramcontent.com/pod-product-compliance
Lightning Source LLC
Chambersburg PA
CBHW071439220526
45469CB00004B/1597